Beyond the Door

A Book of Poems

By Mary Bain

Open Wells Publishing

Also by Mary Bain:-

My Song Matters- a book of poems

Available through lulu.com

Copyright © 2018 by Mary Bain

All rights reserved.

This book or any portion thereof may not be reproduced or used in any manner whatsoever, without the express written permission of the publisher except for the use of brief quotations in a book review or scholarly journal.

ISBN 978-0-244-73818-1

Shilbottle, Alnwick, Northumberland, United Kingdom

Mary Bain   Email:marybain1@hotmail.co.uk

Introduction

I am so happy to be introducing to you my second book of poems!

The last three years have been quite an adventure seeing some big changes, such as our move from London to a village in Northumberland; also an increase in travelling with our ministry (Welcome Network) both in the UK and across Northern Europe.

There have been two more family weddings and the birth of three more grandchildren; making four in total- all boys! This is the backdrop against which these poems have been written.

I have discovered over the years that whenever I want to express my feelings in writing it almost always comes out as a poem! So you will find these poems really do convey some of the ups and downs of my emotions over this time. There are some recurring themes- The Garden in my heart, Coming Home, Seasons and Nature, Stories about Jesus, Family etc. Within the themes some of my struggles can be seen; e.g. Understanding who I am, Loneliness and the empty nest, Needing security, Trusting in God, Healing, Letting go...

However, because many poems arose out of my times spent alone with Jesus, they also bring a message about God's amazing, never-ending love for us, and the intimacy of relationship we can enjoy with Him.

"As I sat, I felt His love for me

It fell down from the ceiling,

Like glittering flakes of silver and gold;

I held out my hands to receive them,

And as they fell

My heart melted within me…"

(from the poem 'An Important Guest')

Some poems are dedicated or inspired by particular people, but please be open to reading them as if they are for you. Where I have written my name, "Mary", put your name there instead.

My hope is that, as you read, you will encounter our Father in Heaven's love for <u>you,</u> and that you will step into that new adventure waiting just for you just <u>beyond the Door!</u>

Mary Bain November 2018

The Front cover shows part of our Prayer Garden, which we have created this year. You are very welcome to come and visit the garden and find a space to draw near to God.

See the Quiet Garden Trust website under the NE section- 'Albafarne', for more information.

CONTENTS

A Garden of Hope

13 The Door of Hope

16 Giving in

19 Summer Breeze

21 In the Garden

23 Gardening

25 Quiet Garden

28 Fall

30 Cultivate Inner Beauty

32 Beyond the Door

The Garden in my Heart

37 Alphabet of Love

39 Beautiful Feet

42 Chosen and Shaped

44 Every Moment

46 Followers

48 Heart Perfume

49 In the Middle

51 Leaving

53 Looking in the Mirror
56 My Home
58 My Song of Love
60 One Flock, One Shepherd
63 Re-Turning and Following
67 Surrender
70 The Living Stone
73 The Oil is Flowing
75 The Perfume of your Presence
78 The Ride
81 This is Worship
84 Try Smiling

Tell me a Story of Jesus

91 An Important Guest
95 Simon's Journey

Welcome Home

103 The Invitation
109 Hospitality
110 Come and See
112 Journey Together

The Family

- 115 Wedding Vows
- 117 Wedding Song
- 121 What's in a Name?
- 123 Father's Joy
- 126 Thank you!
- 129 My Darling
- 131 Bob's Sixty Years
- 135 Empty Nest
- 138 Real Freedom
- 140 Daddy's Heart and my True Home

A Garden of Hope

The Door of Hope

Here is a promise

Hope is a sure thing,

Not a maybe, maybe not

Promises are exciting!

Like an adventure about to unfold-

I can see through the door.

The door is open, and beyond...

There is sunshine and flowers,

Birds are singing,

The sky is blue,

There is a warm breeze blowing,

An invitation to enter in-

A New year;

With a promise of opportunities

To learn, to grow, to explore

With You, Jesus

Walking beside me,

Getting to know You more.

There are challenges too.
So much to learn,
The way to be more like You;
My heart like a garden
Needs some digging,
Turning over of the soil,
Going deeper,
Uprooting the tangles, the confusion
And insecurities,
Laying a steady, rich and faithful foundation –
Your unchanging love for me.

It is good to look back,
To remember Your faithfulness,
Your loving Presence
Constant through the ups and downs
Of the last year.
But I recognise the truth
The need to leave behind
The regrets, the mistakes,
The deliberate turnings away

From You.

Not just mine, but other people's too!

This is a Year of Promise.

I am resolved in this –

Keeping my eyes fixed on You

And with my heart a flutter

At what we can do, together,

I am entering this New Year

Through the door of Hope.

Mary Bain January 2016

(Hosea 2:15 and Lamentations 3:23
You are reassuring me that there is hope. A door of hope. Your mercies are new every day, every morning and great is Your faithfulness)

Giving <u>In</u>

Are you giving up, or giving <u>in</u>?

A seed
Doesn't look very promising
Shrivelled and dry
Wrinkled, pale, insipid
Where is the life in that?

But when you drop it
In to the earth
When you give <u>in</u>
Instead of giving up-
Throwing it away
Or worse-
Leaving it in the packet
Instead of seeing the potential,
The vision,
The picture of what it can become,
Or really is...

When you give <u>in</u>

Then a secret is discovered

<u>In</u> the surrender

Something begins to grow

A life within stirs

In the deepest places

In fact

There is more beneath,

Hidden from sight

Than what people can see

Out in the daylight!

Until, amazingly,

Wonderfully,

Watered and nurtured

And loved by significant others,

A seedling bursts forth

Out of the ground

Resurrection life

Appears

Because the Father,

Who is the Gardener

Loves us always and

Works with us.

He sees, and knows who we are becoming

And is present

With us

Through the challenges

And changes of our lives.

He has not given up on us

Instead He has given <u>in</u>

Given His life.

And on this firm foundation

We are also able to give <u>in</u>

Grow,

And live a very fruitful life.

Mary Bain March 2018

Unless a grain of wheat falls into the ground and dies it remains alone; but if it dies it brings forth much grain. **John 12:24**

And let us not grow weary while doing good; For in due season we shall reap if we do not lose heart (or give up)! **Gal 6:9**

I planted, Apollos watered, but God gave the increase. **1 Cor 3:6**

Summer Breeze

An oak tree stands

Magnificent

What height! What breadth!

Beneath and beyond

A snapshot view-

Straw bales, sun shining down;

I feel the wind blowing my hair,

A gentle soothing breeze;

The drone of a plane high above

And the wind whooshing through,

Shaking and rippling the rustling leaves.

A bee hums past

The grass waving in response,

As I sit silently,

Drinking in the sweetness;

Very faintly, in the distance

Cars are rushing by,

But here

A bird sings,

Just for a moment,

Calling to its mate, perhaps,
A coo of a dove;
Then, a lady's voice calling out.
I sit fascinated, watching;
A dandelion seed floats gently by
Murmurs of meadow movement,
Almost continuous,
Building to a blowing, breezy crescendo...
And falling still again.
I savour the scents of Summer;
What more could we ask for?
Thank you Jesus!

Mary Bain July 2016

In the Garden

You walked with Adam

In the cool of the day

Together,

In the Garden.

I wonder what you talked about?

Did you discuss ways to plant, to prune,

To make the Garden even more beautiful?

Or were you quiet,

Listening to the melodies:

Birds singing their evening praises,

Humming insects,

Or bleating sheep?

Perhaps you felt the soft grass tickling your feet?

The touch of a breeze

Blowing hair across your faces?

I imagine you, sharing the events of your day

Maybe laughing at a joke?

I see you with arms around each other,

Father and son together.

Today, You have entered into my garden,
The hidden garden
In my innermost being.
I am here,
I can hear You calling me,
I yearn to spend time with You!
Just like Adam walked with You
In the beginning of time,
Right now I reach out
To hold Your hand.
And with a thrill in my heart
We walk on through life
Together.

                                              Mary Bain April 2018

Gardening

When we tend our own garden
Pulling out the weeds
That have taken over,
Digging up the beds of earth,
Cutting the grass
And neatening up the edges-
The messy bits,
That look untidy
Frustrating, and difficult to handle;
When we water and feed
The flowers, trying to bloom,
Struggling to survive
When we do this-
We not only benefit ourselves
The blessing spills over for others.
We make a place of beauty
For others to enjoy.
A place to sit

And rest,

To blow bubbles for a baby,

To listen to the birds singing

And to discover

The strawberries of life!

Mary Bain July 2016

Inspired in the early morning after a gardening day, while watching my son, Jonathan, blowing bubbles for little grandson, Edward, to enjoy.

Quiet Garden

The Vegetable Plot

You are the One who satisfies my soul

You are the Living Bread that came down from heaven

Jesus, today, I come to feed on You

You supply my every need

I am hungry for more of You.

Under the Pergola

The path may not always be smooth

But I trust in You to guide me

Flowers spring up, bringing joy and beauty

Delicate, precious;

The walk may be difficult

But there are sweet, sweet moments,

Even in the midst of pain;

Joy persistently breaks through

And above and all around

Your presence shelters me from harm.

The Orchard

I need Your life

I cannot continue trying on my own;

I need You, the Vine.

"Abide, rest, stay in Me," You said,

Here I will stay,

Here I will rest,

Drawing on Your life

To live, myself, and to give to others.

Please cut away what is bad;

I give myself to You again, today,

Thank you that I am alive in You

And You live in me.

I want to bear fruit for Your glory!

The Wood

I keep my roots deep in You

I draw upon your life,

You have a plan for me;

As I spend time with You,

I grow stronger!

Thank you for planting me here;

I am responding to Your nurturing!
This small tree loves Your touch.
Make me part of Your quiet garden
Of peace, refreshment and closeness with You.

The Sheep Field

Thank you, You hear my cry
"My sheep hear My voice"
I keep coming to You
Like the lambs running to their Mummy
You are my El Shaddai;
I feed on Your words.
I am desperate!
Help me , Daddy,
To not try too hard,
But to enjoy the milk
Rest content and full,
Comforted and at peace always,
With You.

Written during a visit to Angerton Walled Garden,
Northumberland.   Mary Bain April 2018

Fall

Softly, gently the leaves are falling

All around me...

Silently I breathe in Your presence

You are at work...

Quietly blowing,

Undressing, removing

Reshaping and recreating

The glowing, burning autumnal figures

Who swirl and display their glorious finery;

Only to lie discarded

Heap upon heap in fading beauty,

Like a once expensive carpet

Soft, under my feet.

Above bare branches reveal

The cold naked truth

Hidden underneath.

I sense Your cleansing

Through and through

A winter resting

Knowing and being known

Waiting in peace.

                      Mary Bain November 2016, Ohio USA

I have always loved Autumn for its colours, scents and fruitfulness; the wonder of many coloured leaves, shiny brown conkers, bonfires, fireworks and fun.

But in this season of life You are teaching me something new.

In the falling away, the taking off and coming out of hiding, the surrender- You gently and persistently help me to see myself- the real me, the naked truth.

And to be at peace in that.

Because You love me and forgive me, Your grace touches me to the core of my being. You have always loved me and You always will!

The glory of the Fall is that it is not the end!

The beauty does not really fade- a bigger, deeper process is going on...

A dying, a resting, a healing...

And then a springing forth anew into a hope-filled future,

enthused with the joy of living life with You, dear Father as Your precious child.

                              Mary Bain November 2016

Cultivate Inner Beauty

Father, You are the Gardener

Who, in the beginning,

Placed Your children in a garden;

Giving them the work of taking care of it.

When they disobeyed You

The consequences shook the very ground

From which they had been formed.

Their task was much harder

But still they laboured on;

Learning the art of cultivation

From You.

Now, Father, you are speaking to me,

Calling forth the very nature of who I am-

To cultivate the beauty of my garden, within.

My garden can be a unique display of beauty;

Like the garden You created in Eden

Full of the colours, scents and

sounds of Your presence.

Alive with wonder and joy-
Showing who You are to the world.
How can I cultivate that inner beauty?
Only by looking
To You.

Father, here I am, standing at attention
My heart adoring my Master.
Without Your grace, where do I begin?
Help me to know how to tend my garden.
To carry a gentle and gracious spirit
To love and forgive,
To make peace wherever I go,
To use my words to bless,
To encourage and to add beauty.
I want to grow a garden which will become
A wonderful meeting place
A lover's hide-away-
For many to find rest
With You.

Mary Bain July 2016

Beyond the Door

Please tell me more about what You want to do in my life!

I feel as if there is a door

I long to walk further, go deeper

There is more to explore

A tunnel of discovery

Where we can come through

To another world

There are joys untold

For us to behold

Never experienced before

Beyond the door.

"Open your eyes, your ears,

Your heart, my child

Use your imagination

Seeing inside...

Do not fear to go forward, My dear

For I am here

My glory shines through

Each step you will take."

I am opening the door
Holding Your hand
And stepping through
I feel the warmth of Your presence
It is clothing me
Sitting silently over my shoulders
Stilling my beating heart
Bringing a confidence
I can do this!

I move forward,
Pushing through the scented branches
The anticipation is overwhelming
Intoxicating, releasing
Glorious, comforting,
Relaxing every bone
With every sense tingling
Alert, in ready expectation
I am stepping forward

You are speaking to me, encouraging,

Showing me more and more!

It is increasing,

My senses reeling,

Until, at last I step out

Walk into the brightness

The glory and joy

Of a shining new adventure

Friendship, flowers and freedom

With You, Jesus,

Forevermore.

                                    Mary Bain July 2018

The Garden in my Heart

Alphabet of Love

Awake, arise, My awesome one, the apple of My eye,
Believe you belong to Me, beautiful you are!
Cuddle close to Me, let Me comfort and caress,
Drink deeply of My love, darling, draw nearer
Enter My embrace!

Feel free to follow My example,
Gaze upon my face,
And in the gazing, may there be a giving;
Holding hands in happiness.

Invite Me into your ideas, imagine and inspire;
Join with Me on a journey to joy
That will never, ever tire!

Kiss Me, O kiss Me quickly
Love Me long and deep;
Melt My heart a million times
Nuzzle nearer, and never leave!

Overwhelmed, I observe you, over and over again;
Passionately you pursue Me,
Quivering with delight, queenly in your frame;
Run with Me, run with Me, My regal one
Surrender, I am speaking out your name!

Tell Me the truth about the two of us,
A tale deserves to be told,
Understand I will love you always
Even when you are old!

Vanquished, My heart is conquered,
As, unveiled My bride appears,
Walking in white towards Me,
While I wipe away My tears.

Ecstatic in My excitement,
I extend My hand and heart,
Yearning only to be united, My beloved,
Zipped together, never more to part!

Mary Bain September 2018

Beautiful Feet

I am holding open the door

The door into the garden

The garden which is my heart;

And I am so eager

To feel the print of Your Feet,

Firmly pressing down the soft grass,

Caressing the wide open flowers,

Touching the tear drops

Clinging to their stems,

Enjoying the intimacy of walking in my garden.

I am feeling Your love for me;

Jesus, You are oh so welcome!

I lie still as I receive You,

My heart is ready to feel again.

As I invite You deeper within,

I become aware of a pain,

Something torn and ragged,

A hole, left ravished by Life's hurts.

What can I do?
My heart is aching;
I hear You say, "Allow Me to mend it."

I think about the cross;
How You took upon Yourself
All that is wrong,
All that is bad,
The pain, the mess, the shame, the sin;
Then I realise
It is the cross You are using
To mend my heart.
I hold it over my pain,
Clinging tightly,
As You gently and tenderly stitch together
The hole, and make it well.

I remember the worst times in my life,
The things I hide from;
Harsh, angry words lying buried
Subconsciously, at the back of my mind;

I deliberately recall those dark days

Carrying them to Your cross;

I allow You to take them

My very worst moments-

Things I have done,

Or others have done to me;

You are transforming them

Into my greatest victories!

I am so thankful dear Lord,

For all that You have done.

Please keep coming to walk in my garden

I want to hear Your voice,

Feel Your beautiful feet,

Enjoying the stroll.

I see the scars from the nails

And I remember the cross

I cry out, "I too am crucified!"

And together, we walk on,

Carrying the good news to the world.

Mary Bain June 2017

Chosen and Shaped

I have opened a door

Come, walk through it with Me.

You have asked Me to change Your heart;

I am doing so.

I am taking and shaping

And forming your heart;

I am washing it,

Sluicing out the debris,

Going deeper than ever before,

And I am polishing you, My daughter;

I am causing you to shine

With My light and My love!

My Name is glorious;

I have written My Name

Upon you!

When people see you

They will see Me too.

You do not lose your identity,

But your identity is made clear-

It is found,

When you allow Me to live in you.

I am loving the home you have made

For Me;

And I am holding you up,

My beautiful glass vase,

Holding you up,

So that many can see

<u>Who I have chosen and shaped you to be;</u>

You are beautiful in your surrender!

As you continue to wait,

I continue to shape you

With My love.

Can you feel My love all around?

My approval in your giving of yourself to Me?

(Yes I can feel it and I love You Daddy, Jesus, Holy Spirit!)
                                        Mary Bain June 2017

Every Moment

I was made to worship You

It comes naturally-

Or supernaturally, perhaps?

Like the flowers that pour out their scent,

As they open up to the warmth of the sun.

Like the birds that lift up their voices

In splendid notes of love;

As they awaken the dawn

And salute the rising of the sun.

Like the bees humming along,

As they visit each flower,

Taste the sweet nectar, then fly away home.

So, in my day of hectic pancake cooking

As well as exciting and interesting conversations

Of loving friendship and drinking coffee,

Of silent giving of myself to You, in prayer,

I worship You.

Every Moment was made for worship;

And I am loving spending my life ,
Just worshipping You!

(Written on Pancake Day)   Mary Bain February 2018

Followers

I am a follower of Jesus

That means I am living like Him.

I am looking at Jesus

Beholding Him in wonder

And I am being changed,

Transformed,

To become like Him.

I take up my cross each day;

But that is my purpose,

What I am here to do.

Just as Jesus came to die

To give His life

To love sacrificially

I, too, am following in His steps.

My purpose is to love,

Giving myself,

All of me;

Just as Jesus did.

It is not a hardship,

It is a joy to love,

To give.

When I am following Jesus,

I know the way,

And I know my purpose.

I understand and experience real love.

To live is to give

And to give is to love-

Real love, not just words,

But truly living a life of love;

Followers find freedom

From selfish preoccupation

And walk openly as sons of the Father,

Enjoying favour in all they do;

Just like Jesus.

                              Mary Bain August 2016

Heart Perfume

Fully participate

In giving myself

In worship

This is how I was created

Shaped with a desire to pour forth

My whole being

In selfless praise

Thanking my God and Saviour

For His unending love

Love which continues

Constant all the way through

My heart bursts forth today

To grow and blossom

A flower

Vibrant and glowing

So happy to be picked

And held in the hand

Of the One

Who gave <u>His life</u> for me.

Written at David's Tent　　　　　　　　Mary Bain August 2016

In the Middle...

In the middle of the sea
In the middle of the night
In the middle of a storm
Jesus comes.
Jesus is there with us,
No need to be afraid,
He has come.
His presence makes all the difference.

In the middle of difficulty
Before things change
The storm is still raging
All around;
We can step out of the boat
Experience amazing miracles,
Do something impossible,
Walking on the water with Jesus.

In the middle of our fear

When everything has gone wrong
Sinking in the depths
Overwhelmed and unable even to see;
He hears our cry for help,
Instantly, we feel His hand
Lifting us into peace;
The storm has ceased in His embrace.

In the middle of our lives,
Our everyday, working existence;
In difficulty, despair or fear
We find Him with us.
We can rise above the problems,
In spite of the storm,
Walking on the impossible,
Trusting even when we doubt and fail;
His hand holds us steady and calm
And we sail on, smiling through the day!

                                      Mary Bain November 2018

Leaving

What does it mean to leave and move on?

A whole mix of emotions

Thankfulness, but also stress,

Joy and hope, but also tears and fears

And how do I cope

With the leaving?

Growing old- truth to be told

I still feel so young inside!

Always a learner and

Even in weakness and fragility,

Knowing it is a fruitful place to be-

In the leaving.

Yet I wish I was different!

I would love to express

The warmth, the delight,

The joy I feel when I'm with my family.

I don't want to leave

The ones I hold so dearly to my heart.
So why are we leaving?

Yes, I have heard a call to move on
A new beginning and
I will do my utmost to carry with me
My family
Even with the distance between us.

Help me, Jesus, to hold them
Expand my heart to keep them
Always in prayer
Always on my mind
Always dear to me;
And to know
Beyond a shadow of a doubt
That Your love is a Home, sweet home,
Where we are always together,
And there is no more leaving.

Mary Bain May 2017

Looking in the Mirror

I am looking in the mirror
What do I see?
I see that I am known
Not forgotten;
My Daddy knows everything about me.

I am looking in the mirror
I feel alone and small,
Things are getting in the way
Yet, of this I am sure
 Your love outshines them all.

I keep looking in the mirror
Who am I, who shall I be?
You show me I am Your child
When I spend time with You
People see You in me.

I look again in the mirror

What am I wearing?
What have You given me?
Your glory is my outfit;
We are one in unity.

I am looking in the mirror
Now, who do I see?
I see someone who can make it
More than a conqueror,
That's me!

I look closely in the mirror,
Someone old looks back at me.
"Look deeper", You say,
"I make all things new,
It's the inner beauty I see!

Keep looking in the mirror
Don't forget what you see,
Listen, My child to My words of love
I am calling forth

Your identity.

When you look in the mirror
It's My glory that you see
I am transforming you
From glory to glory
Until you look just like Me!

Look in the mirror clearly
Then go out and be
A light, shining in the darkness
Known, loved and powerful,
Telling the world about Me."

                                        Mary Bain October 2018

My Home

Where is My home Mary?
Your home is in my heart, Jesus.
Where is My home Mary?
Your home is in my heart, Jesus.
Where is your home Mary?
My home is in <u>Your</u> heart, Jesus.

Where You go, I will go.
Where You stay, I will stay;
And there I will make my dwelling.

Abide in Me, Mary
Find your rest in Me.

You are so welcome in my heart, Jesus,
The door is open,
The welcome mat is laid out,
The kettle is on;

And I am ready to sit down with You,

I am ready to rest at Your feet,

I am ready to hear what You are saying.

I am leaning on Your chest,

Loving Your closeness,

The smell of Your presence

And learning to stay in peace.

Even when the day ahead is busy

And my time is in demand

I can find that place of quiet rest

At home with You, Jesus.

Mary Bain May 2017

My Song of Love

Come fly

Up high

With Me.

There's always more

When you soar

Up above.

Lift your eyes

My dove

Feel My love.

Come and see

Like Me

With eyes of love.

No fear

Dwells here

With Me.

There is rest

In My nest of love.

As we meet, listen to the beat

Of My heart;
My part and your part,
But never apart.
Loneliness leaves
When you receive
My love.

Free to give,
A life to live;
Generosity
Sees Me
Alive in you
In all you do.
Give and give,
Goodness will flow,
At last they will know
Who I am.
They will listen and take in
My song of Love
As <u>you</u> sing over them.

Mary Bain July 2017

One Flock, One Shepherd

Jesus, help me to love the other sheep.
We are all part of Your fold, Your flock.
No one is greater, better or lesser than another;
You know all our names-
You call us by them,
You bring us together;
Not one is forgotten by You.

You search for us,
When we have wandered and are lost,
Far away from the fold.
You do not rest until
We are found and gathered up
Into Your arms;
Restored again, back in the fold.

Daddy, Jesus- Good Shepherd,
I want to be gathered in the sheepfold,

However noisy, uncomfortable,
Or difficult it may be!
Because sheep can be very silly at times!
Naughty too;
And that includes me!

Holy Spirit, keep a careful watch over us,
Like the clever sheepdog
Anticipates ways the sheep may wander,
Moves into the gap,
Keeps them on track,
Together and obedient
 Responding to the Shepherd's call.
We really need Your help!

Together, we are coming to know You-
Our good Shepherd;
Leading us,
Loving and protecting us
Declaring whose we are,
With Your Name.

We are on display to the watching world;

A happy band of believers

Hearing Your voice,

Moving as ONE!

This is Life as it was meant to be,

For all eternity!

One flock, one Shepherd,

In Love and together, forever!

                                        Mary Bain August 2017

Re- turning and Following

Do not forget Me

Return to Me

Come often into My presence

I am here for you.

I am strong on your behalf.

I am opening up the way for you.

But keep returning-

Re- turning;

Do it often;

Turn towards Me every hour!

And every hour, I will be there for you,

Imparting peace.

My grace is sufficient-

More than enough to meet

Every need of yours, and of those

You are helping.

It is My words you are able to speak

My hands you can stretch out to heal
Doing signs and wonders,
Because you and I are one.
No need to feel condemned
My mercy means
I respond to your need full stop!

You shall be my witness, Mary
You shall display My glory.
Be careful not to think it is yours.
Remember we did not come to be served,
But to serve, and to give our lives
A ransom for many.
Like Master, like servant.
Follow Me, follow the Master,
Be like Me, imitate Me
Others will be drawn to Me
Through your life

Oh Jesus, I want to follow You
Please help me to see You;
To be close to Your garment,

To feel the brush of Your cheek,
The breath of Your mouth,
The scent of Your perfume!
I long to be enfolded,
Wrapped around in Your garment-
At peace in Your loving arms.

I see You kneeling
At the feet of the disciples-
The towel around Your waist;
Washing the hot and dusty feet,
Massaging them gently,
As you hold their gaze intently,
Looking and loving the one
In front of You.

Give me the capacity
The breadth of ability
To love, as You love
To serve, to encourage, to comfort and to endure;
I am a follower of Jesus
I will not deviate from this!

This sheep knows where her home is-
With her Shepherd.

                                        Mary Bain May 2016

Surrender

(Mt.11:28-30)

You are showing me the way of surrender

I can lay down my burdens,

Everything falling at Your feet.

Only You

It is only You I long for,

Only You.

I give myself, my needs, my failings;

"Keep bowing your head, Mary

There is joy in taking the yoke

Beside Me."

When I lower my head

And agree that Your will,

Not mine, be done

I find my soul is washed over,

Flooded with peace;

There is no need to worry,

No reason to fear,

Because I am held, kept safe
With You.

I feel the warmth of Your love
Within, and all around me,
Sometimes so intense...
And I know it is Your love
Burning inside me.
I am asking You to break my heart
So that my heart is like Yours.
Open, vulnerable, compassionate and feeling
Not distant, remote, detached and cold,
Like my heart more naturally would be!

If my heart is broken,
The warmth of Your love,
The light of Your goodness,
The image of Your being
Can shine forth,
As I surrender-
Giving myself to You, in love,

Your glory flows from my life.

O, the wonder of being part of Your plan!

Together, holding out the invitation-

"Come, come to Jesus,

Come meet Your loving Father,

Come be filled to overflowing with His gentle Holy Spirit!"

Jesus, here I am,

Your love slave;

I am setting out with you, today

Please hold my hand.

How can I fear when we are together?

                                    Mary Bain   March 2017

The Living Stone

(1 Peter 2:4-6)

This is security, this is peace

Anchored down, at rest

Knowing my foundation-the Rock;

You do not change

You are consistent and stable

Something I can stand upon

Trustworthy

Lasting for all time

No wavering, no wobbling

No fear

My feet are firmly planted

You are here

For me.

And You do not change

Your love for me does not alter

I can depend upon it

Every day

Foundational to my being

   The Cornerstone of my life.
   Though the storms may rage around me
   Some of my own making
   You remain- no variable
   Not even a hint of turning away
   There You stand
My Father, my Rock, my Lover
And my Friend
The True, the Eternal One.

And You choose me
You wait for me
You invite me and You long for me
To stand next to You –
A little chip off the old block
A stone like You
Built together with others
But solid with You
Consistent like You
And lifted up beside You into
A place of honour

Chosen and precious.

Today, I present myself as a living stone
Impress upon me Your image
That I might live my life
Secure and safe
Knowing exactly who I am
In You.

                                                Mary Bain July 2016

The Oil is Flowing

Where can I go from Your presence?

You have poured out the perfumed oil

And I watch it flowing

Pouring, releasing and restoring

Everything and everyone it touches.

The stopper is pulled off

Bottle tipped up, turned upside down

Like my life with You;

And the oil is flowing.

Oh, the joy released

When the oil is flowing!

Blessing and anointing,

Every part receiving;

Cleansing and healing,

Resting and freeing,

Reaching out, to the furthest places.

It is overwhelming-

The wonder of Your love;

Awakening and reviving
Every part of Your body
From the head to the feet.

So, we unite our hearts
A happy band of brothers
Dwelling together
Beneath this waterfall of blessing.
The dew of Your presence
Is covering us,
Your people;
Carrying Life in all its fullness
And changing this land
Forevermore.

                                        Mary Bain March 2018

(See Psalm 133 "Behold how good and how pleasant it is when brothers dwell together in unity...")

The Perfume of Your Presence

I give You permission to take this pot,
This cracked and weak vessel of my life
With some potential inside;
With gold that shines, softly and gently,
Of more value than I even know,
More than I can comprehend-
Everything I am and have,
You hold it, dear Lord,
In Your beautiful hands;
And I am asking You
To take it
And break it
To smash it to pieces
Because I want to be free
To be
All that You have made me to be!

There is something

In the breaking,

Something in my heart that needs to learn,

To grow, to change

Because I want to feel and express

What You feel, what You express,

Whatever the cost and the pain;

No pain, no gain!

So, dear Jesus, I am crying out

Alongside You-

My personal garden of Gethsemane

"Not my will but Yours be done!"

Break my heart!

I'm taking up my cross,

Show me what it means,

I bow my head low

To be crucified beside You.

Smash this pot!

I so desire that the perfume of Your presence

Invade my life and pour out

All around.

Then please glue me back together,

(I am waiting for You),

So Your glory may shine forth,

Strong and brilliant, forever!

Mary Bain April 2017

The Ride

See, I showed you then
That I am Faithful and True
I am the Strong One
Who carries you through
But closeness is the key
Riding bareback with me
Skin to skin, I carry you
My child
So you can feel my Power
As we ride...

Now I show you again
I am Faithful you see
I know how to heal the pain
You hid so well from Me
It is my nature to be faithful
I will never let you down
Filling every hole
With faith

What was lost is found

But there is still more to know
To smell, to sense, to see
More joy, deeper and stronger
Than you would ever think could be!
Because, I know it too
I share your pain;
The betrayal, the rejection,
And especially the shame;
But you share in My triumph,
And everyone will see
As you ride through life,
Riding bareback with Me.

Together, we're on a journey
The adventure's about to begin
I am calling out-
Will you ride with Me?
Will you ride with Me?
"Yes, yes I will ride!

It's a glorious ride Jesus,
At Your side, following free
Stride by stride,
We're galloping through it all,
Galloping on to victory!"

Mary Bain August 2016

This is Worship

There is a song to sing
Sometimes I must run to catch it
Like a ball of light floating by,
I need to push through
Keep running
To find it;
Always ahead, yet somehow,
Still, within my reach.

All around are the flowers,
Pushing up their soft petals,
Frowsy, a little sleepy
They rise up;
Delicate and vulnerable they appear;
Not just one, but masses
Crowds and clouds of wonder
All around my feet
As I run on
To catch the song-

The song that bounces and bobs along
In front of me.

Sparkling in the sun
A delight of joy
I continue to run
There is so much love
So much strength
As I chase Your embrace
In the song!
It is my life to do this;
Not a small thing
This is what my heart desires-
To keep running,
To keep giving, serving and loving
Surrounded by Your embrace.

The chase is the desire
To be with You
Always,
Forever Yours,

At one and complete

The song is found

As I lay down

And kiss Your feet.

                                        Mary Bain December 2017

Try Smiling

Still and silent, I lay,
Trying to focus,
To look into Your face
It felt forced
Tense and unreal
As if You weren't actually there.

I opened my hands
No holding back now
Access-
That's the key;
My heart bare before You
I waited...
Every sense alert.

"Try smiling," You said,
Such a simple phrase;
"It does make a difference," I thought,
When you meet someone,

You smile and greet."

"Dear one," You said,

"When you smile, it is so sweet"

So I smiled at Jesus,

Father and Holy Spirit, too!

It felt false at first,

But I kept on going, and

You prompted me once or twice,

When the smile slipped away,

Under the bedcovers!

As I smiled, I felt You come,

My whole body rested,

Relaxed and warm.

I enjoyed the feeling,

Like basking in the sunshine

On a Summer's day;

I sensed a deep peace

Washing over me.

Still You encouraged me,
"Keep smiling," You said'
And as I did,
We went a layer deeper
The fire of Your love
Began a cleansing in me;
Fierce, but sweet
Right into my centre,
Melting the very core of my being.

Like a lover
Remembering a caress,
I smiled and smiled
As You worked a change deep within;
Taking the liquid gold,
Picking out the stones-
The bitterness, the jealousy, envy and pain,
You threw them away;
Shaping me well again!

There is nothing between us now,

Joy is flowing through me;

"Look at My hands", I hear You say,

Again I smile when I see

On Your finger, my heart,

Made a circle of gold,

Shining bright!

You are showing me that I can also love like You

I can invite and include others

Into the circle,

Because of what You have done.

I am Your gentle dove,

Feeling Your peace

Together with You;

Joined, as one.

Mary Bain February 2018

Tell me a Story of Jesus...

An Important Guest

The sun was shining through the window,

Beams of warmth falling at His feet

Such Beautiful feet,

Washed and perfumed

At rest, after the long journey.

I sat so close to Him

I could almost reach out and touch them...

But listen,

He was speaking to me!

I raised my eyes to His face.

Immediately, I was entranced

His eyes...

I felt as if I would never want to stop looking

Into His eyes.

Sparkling blue, inviting, teasing and yet,

Full of depth and understanding.

Such love...

'This is where I will stay forever

Just to watch His face,

To listen to His voice,
To bathe in His love.'

In the background
I could hear my sister, in the kitchen
Bustling about,
Looking for the best dishes,
Dropping a spoon,
Sighing a bit.
I felt her frustration with me.
Such an important guest
And I was not helping her!

Yet, I could not move
It was as if there were only me and Him
In the room,
Held, bewitched by His gaze,
Enthralled by His voice,
I was in another world
Time standing still...
As I sat, I felt His love for me
It fell down from the ceiling,

Like glittering flakes of silver and gold.
I held out my hands to receive them,
And as they fell,
My heart melted within me...
Suddenly she came and stood before Him,
Carrying her complaint;
'Lord, don't You care for me?
My sister is not helping me,
I'm doing everything alone
Why don't You tell her to help?'
He turned His face toward her,
I felt the guilt creep up inside,
Blushing at what I had not done.

He spoke very gently to Martha
I knew He appreciated
Her welcoming heart
He said she was getting herself worked up
Missing something better
That only one thing was really needed
And I had chosen to do it...
I looked up at my sister

To see her eyes fill with tears
Getting up,
I hugged her for a long time.
And then we both sat down
At Jesus' feet;
 Dinner could wait!
With hearts and hands open
To receive His love
Together,
We gazed into His beautiful face.

                                        Mary Bain March 2017

(inspired by Luke 10:38-42 and Psalm 27:4)

Simon's Journey

I could tell something was going on,

Even at Passover the streets were not usually so crowded

A seething mass of people

Noisy, and slightly out of control,

Roman soldiers amongst them,

Looking fierce,

Quick to raise their spears,

Threatening and dangerous;

I wondered who the unlucky bastard was

It was clear the crowd was panting for someone's blood,

An execution definitely in the making!

What a contrast to the tranquil morning scene

I had left behind me in the hills!

My wife waving from our door,

My two sons, Rufus and Alexander running beside me,

Till the far gate of our farm,

A last hug, a goodbye, and they were gone

To feed the chickens and watch the sheep,
While I walked on alone to the city,
Hopeful of finding the answer to our problems
That weighed so heavy on my mind...

As I was pondering
The road ahead of me became empty,
People were running away,
Pushing back to the sides of the street,
Until only I was left standing,
Bewildered and confused,
In the middle of the road,
Right next to the Roman garrison.

A man was being dragged out
Through the gates,
Covered in blood and bruises,
A complete mess of humanity,
He staggered under the huge wooden beam
Across his shoulders;
While a mockery of thorns,

Twisted into a crown, graced his head.

I could not take my eyes off him
It was as if time stood still...
He fell heavily in front of me
And reaching down to help him up,
Our eyes met;
A world of emotion was contained in that look
Deep, deep pain and yet beyond,
Above, and piercing through it all
A brightness-
The enduring spark of purest love;
I was moved to the core of my being.

Rough hands were pushing, forcing me,
The soldier in charge shouting in my face
"You, what is your name?
Where are you from?"
"Simon, from Cyrene", I replied.
"You, Simon from Cyrene,
You will now carry this man's cross!"

Before I could say a word
I felt the weight crash on my shoulders,
The man was pulled up
We walked side by side under the beam.
I did not know his name
But I knew I had met the One
I had been looking for.

Our journey was the worst
I have ever experienced.
The vitriol spat out from the crowds,
Who jeered, pushed and mocked us
As we stumbled under the weight of the cross;
He was quiet for a long time,
Then, all at once, He was speaking to me;
"Simon," He said,
If you serve Me, then follow Me,
And where I am, you will be there too,
If you serve Me,
You will be honoured by My Father."
"I want to serve You, always" I replied,

And in that moment,
Even though we still carried the weight of the cross,
I felt a great burden fall off me;
I knew that my family would be ok,
In some way my debts would be cleared
Because of what had happened between us this day-
Me and the Man
I now know to be Jesus.

I stayed to watch Him die,
My heart felt as if it was breaking
But I was sure this was not the end;
Because of His words to me-
"Where I am, you will be also"
I gave Him my heart that day,
And have known His presence with me ever since.
He paid the price for me,
For you, and for all of us.
So please remember the story of how I met Jesus,
He is waiting to meet you too!

Mary Bain March 2018

Welcome Home!

The Invitation

I found it a few days ago

Sorting out things for the move

I had forgotten how big it was

Edged in gold

White card, hand written

Beautiful, carefully crafted,

My personal invitation-

To the Wedding.

Wrapped around it, even still

The soft tissue paper

I had kept, as it had been then,

Covered in hearts, and still carrying

The sweet, lingering perfume

Of His presence...

I pulled it off

And held the card in my hand...

The years rolled away

I was a student again

Sitting on my bed,
A Sunday evening after Mass,
Alone.
My heart aching within me
I had been learning something hard to handle,
It made me feel lonely and afraid,
The man I thought was in love with me
Wanted me to be someone else.

The scene moved forward;
I was drinking coffee
In Bob's new room,
Chatting and laughing,
Feeling excited again
My heart beating fast
As our eyes met and we shared
About the book
He'd been reading that week
Could it really be true?

Then, another scene;
A conversation with Bob's friend, a Christian,

"Did I really know Jesus?" was the question;
"Did I know what He had done for me?"
I thought I did;
I answered all the questions correctly,
Except the last.
Why had no one said this before?
"Had I really given Him my heart?"

Back in my own room again
I read through the leaflet
Bob's friend had given me
It made such perfect sense;
Every word spoke hope and healing
Into my empty, aching heart.
I had been looking for a man
To fill the void inside,
Give me affirmation,
To love me, just as I am.
I discovered Jesus,
Loving me completely, totally,
Even before I was born!

Dying, just for me;
It went far and beyond the love of a man!
Nothing more was needed;
I prayed a simple prayer
And opened my heart to Him...

And that was when I received the Invitation;
As I slept that night,
Jesus walked into my room.
I felt His presence,
His touch on my forehead,
His soft whisper of love,
"Now you are Mine."
In the morning I found the card
On my pillow,
My name written at the top
In gold, and below
Three simple words-
"Come, follow Me!"

And so the Invitation is definitely being packed
With all our belongings

As Bob and I move on today.
The joy found in following Jesus
Continues to grow.
And I know
It was the best decision I have ever made
To give my heart, and live my life,
Forever, with Him.

And yes, the Wedding is still to come,
And the Bridegroom is tenderly calling
To you, dear Reader;
Have you discovered your invitation yet?
He is waiting for you.

                                      Mary Bain   April 2017

The Hospitality of Abraham or The Trinity

(Drawn from the 15th century icon painted by Andrej Rublev)

Father, Son= Jesus, Holy Spirit.

There is a space at the table for YOU!

Hospitality

We have a place at the table

Personally invited into relationship

Into the circle of love

You have shared together

The Three- from the beginning of time!

This is our home-

Father, Jesus, Spirit.

There is so much joy

Life and love-

In giving our love,

Sharing Your love,

Enjoying Your presence

And carrying the joy,

The laughter,

The peace

And the fulfilment, with us

To others.

Your hospitality overwhelms us!

The Circle always includes

One more; Forevermore!   Mary Bain September 2018

Come and See!

Come and see the One
You have been searching for all your life,
He has been looking for you.

Come and see the One
Who already knows all about you
He is calling you by your name.

Come and see the One
Who spoke everything into existence.
He is speaking life over you today.

Come and see the One
Who shines and overcomes the darkness.
He is the Light of the World.

Come and see the One
Gentle and pure as a Lamb,
He gives Himself for you and takes away all your sins.
Come and see! Come and see!

He is inviting you into His home.
Come and see!
If you only meet Him
Look into His face
You will never want to be anywhere else,
Only to stay with Him,
Always.

Come and see!
He asked me to bring you.
He is longing to meet you.
He wants to spend time
<u>With you.</u>
Come and see the One...

Mary Bain April 2018

(For Margaret.)   See John Chapter 1

Journey Together

Let's not go back to where you were,

Or even travel to where I am now,

Let's journey on together

To a new place of welcoming love,

Where we both have learnt to love better;

Where we have come to know,

To reflect,

And to others show

The truth of who God is-

The amazing breadth

Of His heart-breaking love,

For this needy, dirty,

But extremely wonderful world

In which we live!

Mary Bain June 2018

The Family

Wedding Vows
For Dave and Holly

I lift my veil

We stand face to face,

Nothing hidden,

Looking into each other's eyes.

There is a hush of expectancy,

A pause of anticipation

Then, in <u>hope,</u> we repeat the familiar responses.

I give you my hand in marriage.

I feel the warmth of yours,

As we hold each other.

Looking down at the circles of gold-

No end and no beginning,

In <u>faith</u>, we promise

To love each other, always.

We speak out our vows in stumbling solemnity-

"To have and to hold, for better, for worse...

All that I am, I give to you

All that I have, I share with you...

Till death do us part."

I cannot imagine you old, but

Amazingly in this moment I find

My heart, joined together with yours

In a <u>love</u> that is sealed and strengthened

With a lingering kiss!

"These three remain always- faith, hope and love, but the greatest of these is love"

Mary Bain   June 2016

A Wedding Song

Love's Beginning

It all begins in a garden

A garden full of life and colour

Bursting with brilliance and light

Scents and smells

Goodness and fruitfulness

Filled with a peaceful Presence

And bringing purpose and order,

In the care and keeping of it.

And in the garden, a man who is lonely.

No bird or animal can fill the gap within his heart

Although many are brought to him

And he gives names to them all.

Until a marvelous miracle occurs

A part of him is taken, while he sleeps

And when he awakes

He finds standing before him

The most beautiful creature of all-

A woman, who just fills and completes his life.

And the wedding bells ring out for the first time,

As two become one in marriage!

Love's Song

Today, let's listen to their love song,

The Bridegroom is singing it now

and has been throughout the years.

We can just catch the strains of the melody-

'Come away with me' he sings

'My beautiful one,

All of me loves all of you,

All your curves and all your edges

All your perfect imperfections...

Don't go changing to try to please me

Girl, you're amazing,

Just the way you are!

And now the bride joins in,

'Blow upon my garden of spices my lover,

Je t'aime...

Your gentleness has captured my heart,

I give my all to you....'

Love's Future

Looking forward into the future-
A new beginning, a city shining with light.
Here is the Bridegroom,
Wooing each one of us to Himself.
He is full of love for His beautiful bride.
Constant and faithful,
Choosing only to see the best in her.
She has made herself ready,
And is longing to be with Him.
The invitations are sent to everyone,
No one is forgotten.
A magnificent banquet is laid out
And the Bridegroom and His bride are calling,
'Come and drink!'
The wine is flowing in a never-ending stream
And there is a place for each of us at the table.
Let's choose to take part, and enter in
As the wedding bells ring with joy
And two <u>forever</u> become One in marriage.

Mary Bain April 2016

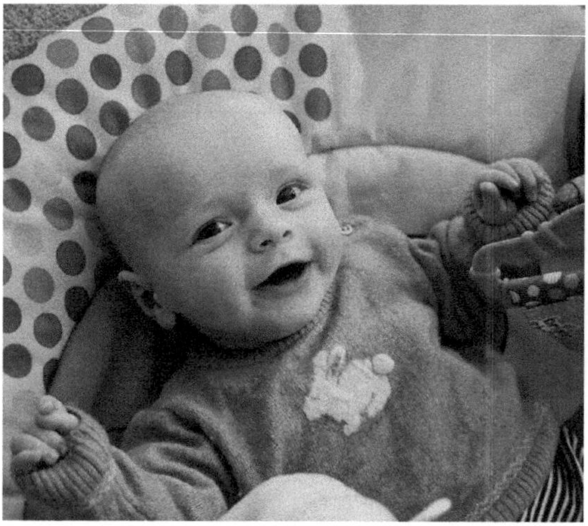

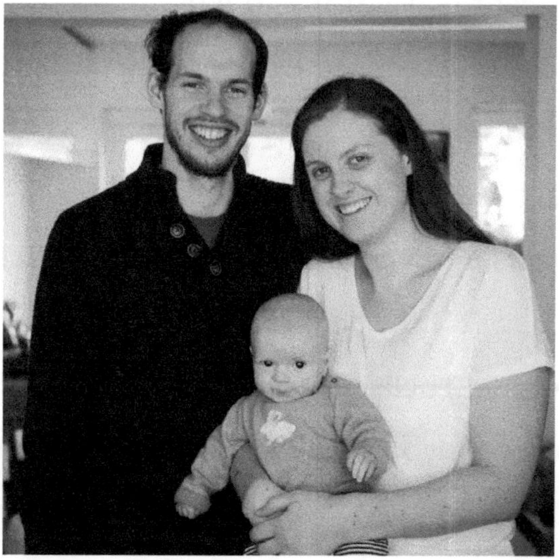

What's in a Name?

Hello world, here I am,

Alexander Joshua Bain.

My name is important

Chosen specially for me

Perhaps I should explain...

Alexander- because, though small

I'm really GREAT-

I can fight any battle and win!

I will not give up

I know that God's love

Is keeping me safe

All around, and deep within.

Joshua is my middle name

He was a fighter too!

Like him, I want to be brave and strong

Lead others, and do what God says,

So God's power will be seen as walls fall down,

Evil destroyed, when Love walks in.

Joshua means the same as Jesus,
I'm so happy He is also in my name!
Jesus risked everything to save the lost ones,
Gave His life for even little old me!
I feel the challenge to grow up like Him
Become all that God has called me to be!

So, here I am, Alexander Joshua,
My life so far has been really fun,
I have learnt to trust my parents
I feel secure, I can depend on them.
There is peace and contentment,
No pressure to perform;
I am loved, just as I am.
Today, I hope you see something in me,
And that you will discover the same,
As you rest in the Father's love for you,
Hidden deep inside <u>your name</u>.   Mary Bain May 2018
For Alexander Joshua on the occasion of his dedication

Father's Joy

Abigail,

How can I describe the joy

The blessing

The sweet perfume

that you are in our lives?

So true to your name,

"Father's joy",

Like a flower, opening up to the sun.

It has been a privilege,

An honour,

To watch you grow,

To see your delicate and sweet tenderness,

The fragility which could easily feel hurt,

Develop and blossom

Into someone, who bears the fruit

Of strong, enduring friendships with many,

Including us, your parents!

There is a sweetness you express

In both words and actions,

Beautiful to behold.

The little girl who loved to be with her brothers and sisters,

looking through animal books,

playing Mouse-trap,

drawing cute, curvy people

that were us- the family,

always surrounded by hearts and flowers!

The teenager who sang and danced,

created delicious and dangerous cakes,

often helped, without being asked

and always wanted to get cosy beneath the blanket-

You have grown into this caring and compassionate woman,

Whom we love so very much!

We stand amazed at what our Father God has done,

Excited too, at what is still to come!

There is so much more to express,

To explore,

As we give ourselves in love to Him,

And to those He has placed around us.

So be encouraged, dear daughter,

To keep opening up

Singing out your unique song of love.

In weakness and vulnerability,

His strength is most clearly seen.

Keep smiling too,

You bring so much joy into our lives.

Now, receive, yourself

And bask in the warmth of His

(and our) approval,

Smiling down on you.

Mary Bain March 2018

(For Abigail with love on her 22nd Birthday.
"Come on and smile, come on and smile!
Make it last a long while!
God gave you your smile!")

Thank you!

Thank you for seeing the impossible
And reaching out for it;
For stretching and believing
For more than you can see
Around you now!

Thank you for inspiring me,
With a vision
That we can go somewhere
Together.

Thank you for delving into God's word
Digging for treasure,
Reaching for more
Further up and further in!
I love the excitement of life
With you.

Thank you for being a loving husband and father,
Encouraging, comforting,

Listening and believing
In me, in us;
In each of our children.

The sparkle and spontaneity;
I am enjoying the adventure,
As our boat bobs onwards,
With the sun shining on us
And the peace of His presence
Holding us safe, always.

For Bob on Father's Day   Mary Bain June 2016

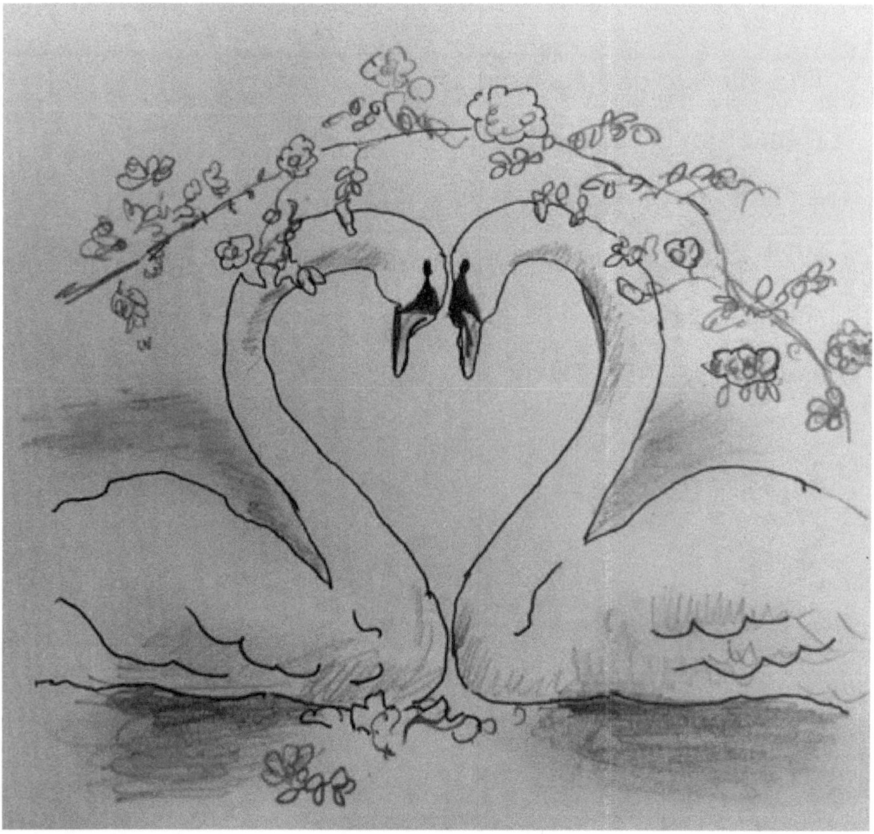

My Darling

I love the way this picture
Shows a heart of love
Clearly seen and on display
When two separate and unique birds
Come together face to face.

My life and yours held together
As we embrace
Eyes fixed on each other
Heart joined as one.

Thank you Father for my husband
As much a gift today
As the day we married
And much more loved and appreciated
Thank you for bringing us together,
For joining us together,
And keeping us together.

And thank you my darling,

For giving yourself to me!

Mary Bain 7th July 2016

Bob- Sixty years

Sixty years to celebrate

My dear Husband,

A third before I knew you,

Two-thirds of life together.

I have always loved the sound of your voice, (A good thing really)

And it has been quite an adventure as we stepped out together;

The day I walked down the aisle

And stood beside you to say our vows,

It was serious – but I felt such joy!

I could not stop smiling,

So much so that my face ached!

The day whirled by in a bubble of excitement,

Which will never be forgotten!

Getting to know someone takes time,

And it hasn't finished yet!

No pretending – there have been some difficult moments;

When I wondered where to turn,

Who I was, what to do...

But I am certain there were times like this for you too,

And amazingly and wonderfully,

Our God, our loving Daddy

And our friend and brother, Jesus

Have pulled us through!

He has given us His strength,

Patience and kindness,

To keep going, to keep loving,

And to keep serving each other.

So I am here to say "Thank you" today,

Just for being you!

You are so dear to me

Our hearts are entwined together.

We have learnt a lot about each other

So much so – we even tell one another's jokes!

We have survived, even triumphed,

Through the busy years

Of raising a much loved and precious bunch of Bains!

And now here we are –

Still loving each other,

Still enjoying deep discussions,

Singing together,

Tramping through the fields of life;

Listening to the birds,

And smelling the roses

You keep buying me!

(Don't stop by the way!)

I know you more, and love you more

Today, than that day we met

In the Upper Coffee Lounge, Sheffield Student's Union

But I also know that there is still more to know,

And many more adventures to come together:

And I'm excited for our future,

The changing seasons-

Becoming Grandparents,

As well as Mum and Dad,

Husband and Wife...

Thank you for all the encouragement

You have given me!

God has stuck us together

Like the stamp and the letter,

And I am up for the journey-

Together, we are going places!

                                    Mary Bain 22nd October 2017

Empty Nest

How full is your nest?

If someone has gone,

How much do you miss them?

If your nest is still half full,

Do you feel happy?

Can you feel happy

When the nest is completely empty?

When Life leaves you alone?

Does God understand

How it feels to have an empty nest?

Does it help to know

He may feel it too?

When Adam and Eve left the garden

Do we remember His cry?

"Adam, Adam, where are you?"

When He hung on the cross,

Can we remember what He shouted out?

"My God, My God, why have You forsaken Me?"

God is also a parent,
If His heart is breaking for His children
To come back home,
What does that mean for us?
Is there something to learn from the Empty Nest?
I think there is!
When you love, it hurts, and
We were made to live in Family;
 Father is yearning,
Aching for His children;
Like us, (or is it-we, like Him?)
He misses them a lot!

Jesus speaks about it in a parable;
The Father looks out every day,
Waiting for the lost son to come home,
He does not give up
His love is consistent,
He is patient but not passive,
He waits in prayer,

Ready to run as soon as He sees him;
He accepts him, just as he is,
Receives him,
Holds nothing against him,
Forgives, and lavishes His love on him;
There is restoration and rejoicing,
And the Father embraces the son,
Holding him close to His heart.

Father, help us to handle our empty-nest,
To learn from You and love our children
The way that You love us.

Mary Bain February 2018

Real Freedom

You are free to love
Free to be
All that you choose to be
Free to live
Free to grow
To say "Yes" and even say "No"!

I lay down any claim,
Which may have restrained,
Held you back, or tied you down
For love is not love
If forced from above
But is found when a life is laid down.

A mother's joy is very sweet
Despite the toil and often heart-rending pain,
Truly I surrender the best bit of me,
When I sow my life-seed in His Name.

Here I lie, no longer I,

But Christ, living His life in me.

The seed has died, but multiplied,

Many sons and daughters do I see,

Serving Jesus, knowing truth,

Free to live, free to love, free to be!

                                        Mary Bain May 2018

Jn 15:3 Greater love has no man than this...

Jn 12:24 Unless a grain of wheat falls...

Jn 8:36 Therefore if the Son sets you free, you shall be free indeed.

Gal 2:20 I am crucified with Christ. It is no longer I that live...

(For my adult children)

Daddy's Heart and my true Home!

Daddy, Your heart is so big!
There is so much to explore
Within Your heart.
I am excited to be in my new home
With You!

Every room in My heart, dear one,
Is filled with My love;
But also with the wonders
Of your own life-
You can live it again,
Remember, and be thankful,
For I have shared it with you,
And have loved you
Through it all!

I don't know how to write this poem-
I have been thinking about this;

That my home,

My true Home is in Father's heart.

I thought about the size of His heart;

All it contained,

As pertained

To His relationship with me.

It seemed like His heart was a bit like our new home!

Big, many rooms,

Different places to explore,

Corners to sit,

Places to be at peace-

To look, to relax,

To chat as friends,

Eat, sleep and love.

It felt like Father's heart held

All the precious, sweet moments

Of my life,

Because He had experienced them too,

Together with me!

Father was there, when I ran through the fields,

As a little girl;

When I stopped to gather cowslips into bunches,
When Ma was pushing me on the swing,
Higher and higher,
Till it felt like I was flying in the sky!
When I sat next to my Daddy
At the dinner table,
Father was there too,
As my Daddy plaited my hair,
Like he used to plait the manes of the horses
At his farm, years before..
Every room in Father's heart
Holds different memories
For me to live again, and explore.

I can revisit those early morning hours,
Walking home,
Holding hands with Bob,
Giddy with the blossoming of new love;
Sharing a sweet and funny moment,
As a hedgehog shuffled by,
Surprising and delighting us!

Or relive the fun of two little boys,
Dressing up and running down the path
To meet Daddy,
As he arrives home from work;
Experience again the activity of little hands
Pushing pastry into shapes beside me,
As I make dinner for the family.

I see myself in the garden
Hanging out the washing,
(As I loved to do with my Mummy)
Now laughing, and getting cross sometimes,
As little girls stretch up to peg out the clothes,
Inevitably dropping some in the mud!
Oh, but the chaotic joy
As we dash out to snatch it in again,
When we realize it is raining!
Sweet, sweet moments!

Then there are other rooms,
Where the joy is mixed with pain-
Small, sad glimpses;

Sitting with my arm around a teenage son
As we cry together over a special rabbit.
Scary moments of wrenching love-
I wave goodbye to another son,
As he disappears into the operating theatre,
Not knowing if I will see him again.
Tears and fears flowing on another difficult day,
As I drive the car to bring the kids home from school
And try to handle some painful news.

All this, mixed with the hilarious fun of movies together,
Under the blanket
With my growing-up girls;
And cosy bedtime stories, all through the years!
Father's heart contains it all;
I am so glad it is so,
Because this is my home
My real home;
My life with Jesus, Father and Holy Spirit-
It contains all these memories-
The good, the bad, the sad,

The funny, the surprising,
The ordinary and extraordinary,
The wondrous and the miraculous!
They have not disappeared,
I am happy I can revisit them;
Relive, appreciate, be thankful,
Enjoy them again.
No worries, no regrets,
All is at peace, all is forgiven;
It has been worth it!
Every room is full of Father's Love,
And His Love covers it all.

                                        Mary Bain   July 2017